101 Pageant Interview Questions for the Young Contestant

JULIETTE EDWARDS

ISBN: 1976422655
ISBN-13: 978-1976422652

DEDICATION

This book is dedicated to all of the pageant mamas out there helping their girls become the best contestants, leaders, and ladies the world will ever see.

ACKNOWLEDGMENTS

A special thanks to all of the pageant directors, coaches, moms, fellow contestants, and pageant little sisters who have helped shape me into the strong, confident woman I have become through your undying support, friendship, mentorship, and inspiration. My crowns don't just belong to me, they belong to the team who supported me through all of my wins, losses, practices, tears, exhaustion, and pride.

101

PAGEANT INTERVIEW QUESTIONS FOR THE YOUNG CONTESTANT

Interview is one of those pageant events that contestants either love or hate. There are many more fans of the gown competition than interview. Why? It's easier to feel your best with hair (and sometimes make-up) done to the 9's in a sparkly princess gown.

Interview, on the other hand, is done behind a closed door without mom's encouraging glances in a more stuffy outfit. However, it's also one of the most important events, particularly in scholarship pageants such as National American Miss, Miss American Coed, International Junior Miss, and Miss America.

What kinds of questions will they ask your Princess, Sweetheart, Jr. Pre-Teen or Junior Princess contestant? Judges at these pageants keep the political questions to the older age groups and focus more on everyday life questions for the youngest contestants.

Take some time and see how your princess handles the questions in this book. Help her learn to avoid 1-word answers. Instead of "Yes", have her answer "Yes, because…".

Practicing answers can give your young contestant more confidence in the interview room without you!

1.

What is your favorite color?

2.

What is your favorite activity in school?

3.

What is your favorite toy?

4.

What is your favorite TV show?

5.

Do you have any pets?

6.

What is your favorite food?

7.

What is your favorite song?

8.

What do you like to do for fun?

9.

If you could meet any cartoon character, who would you want to meet?

10.

What is your favorite animal at the zoo?

11.

What is your favorite book to read?

12.

If you could get one wish, what would you wish for?

13.

What is your favorite treat?

14.

Do you have any brothers or sisters?

15.

Tell me something about you
that makes you really special?

16.

If you cooked dinner for me,
what would you make?

17.

What is your favorite game to play?

18.

Tell me about your family?

19.

What is your favorite drink?

20.

Which holiday do you like best?

21.

Do you have a favorite movie?

22.

Who is your favorite singer?

23.

Do you like to play "dress up"?

24.

Who is your favorite cartoon character?

25.

What fun things do you like to
do with your family?

26.

If you could go anywhere in the
world, where would you go?

27.

What is your happiest memory?

28.

Why do you like being a kid?

29.

What makes you strong?

30.

Other than your mom & dad,
who helps take care of you?

31.

Can you tell me a funny story?

32.

What's the grossest thing you can think of?

33.

Tell me about your favorite pet.

34.

If you were a superhero, who
would you be?

35.

What makes you happy?

36.

What is the nicest thing you
have ever done for someone?

37.

What is your favorite snack?

38.

What do you like to do with
your mom?

39.

How did you get ready for the pageant?

40.

What do you want to be when
you grow up?

41.

What makes you proud?

42.

Who do you talk to when you have a problem?

43.

Who is your favorite singer?

44.

What was your favorite family vacation?

45.

What is your favorite thing about school?

46.

If you could be a Disney
Princess, which one would you
like to be?

47.

What makes you sad?

48.

What is your favorite thing to play?

49.

Who is your best friend?

50.

If you could live anywhere in the world, where would you live?

51.

What makes you special?

52.

What do you do to cheer up a
friend who is sad?

53.

If you could have any animal as
a pet, what would it be?

54.

What is the most exciting thing
you have ever done?

55.

What is something you like about your mom?

56.

Do you like competing in pageants?

57.

What do you like to do with
your dad?

58.

Who is your favorite teacher?

59.

What is your name and how do you spell it?

60.

What is something nice that
you've done for a friend?

61.

What was your favorite part of the pageant so far?

62.

If I gave you $1, what would you
do with it?

63.

Can you tell me about your
favorite color?

64.

If you had a magic wand, what
would you ask for?

65.

Do you play any sports?

66.

What is the best thing that has
ever happened to you?

67.

What makes you laugh?

68.

What is your favorite thing
about being a girl?

69.

Who is your favorite person and why?

70.

If I came over to your house to
play, what would we do first?

71.

What makes someone beautiful?

72.

What have you done to make
someone happy?

73.

Tell me about yourself.

74.

Who is your role model?

75.

Would you rather wear a dress
or pants?

76.

What does your mom or dad do
that makes you happy?

77.

What is your favorite holiday?

78.

What was the last book you read?

79.

If you were an animal what kind
of animal would you be?

80.

What do you do after school?

81.

Who is your favorite teacher?

82.

Describe your best friend.

83.

Tell me the name of one of the
other girls at the pageant that
you like and why you like her.

84.

If someone makes you mad,
what do you do to calm down?

85.

If you were going to get only
one present for your birthday,
what would you want it to be?

86.

Who is your favorite superhero?

87.

Who is your favorite movie star?

88.

What is one thing you can't wait
to do when you're older?

89.

What is your favorite song?

90.

What do you like to do in the summertime?

91.

What is the hardest thing about being a kid?

92.

Do you like to help other people?

93.

What kind of music do you like?

94.

What makes a good friend?

95.

Do you have a nickname?

96.

What is the best gift/present
you've ever been given?

97.

What is your favorite smell?

98.

Do you know any jokes?

99.

What is your favorite color to wear?

100.

What is your favorite flavor of ice cream?

101.

Which Disney Princess is most like you?